Killifreth Mine

and

Early Mining at Chacewater

by

Allen Buckley

Penhellick
Publications

First Published by Penhellick Publications, Pool,
Camborne, Cornwall

Copyright 2011 J.A. Buckley

ISBN 978 1 871678 71 0

Front Cover photograph: General view of Killifreth enginehouses
in July 1979. Photo by Tony Clarke.

Grateful thanks to Tony Clarke for the use of his extensive
collection of photographs.

Printed and bound for Penhellick Publications
by R Booth Ltd
The Praze, Penryn, Cornwall TR10 8AA

Contents

Group of Killifreth miners before The Great War

INTRODUCTION

ALONGSIDE the main road between Chacewater and Scorrier stand the gaunt remains of Killifreth tin mine. The ruins of four enginehouses and several other mine buildings stretch in line along the strike of the principal lodes, in mute witness to the centuries of toil in the rock below. The grandeur and elegance of Hawkes Shaft enginehouse has become a symbol of a once-great local mining industry. Repaired and renovated in the 1980s, the enormous house and tall, slender chimney stack, stand before a background of trees in a setting which could hardly be improved by art. Killifreth, appropriately, means 'dappled wood' or 'grove', in the Cornish language.(1)

Yet, Killifreth was never an important mine. All around were mines which dwarfed her. In comparison with Wheal Busy, Poldice, United and Consolidated mines, the numbers employed at the mine and the production of minerals, were very small. Despite this, Killifreth was a much more typical Cornish mine than any of its great neighbours. The limited extent of its sett, the relatively shallow depth of its workings, the sporadic periods of working, the modest tonnages of ore hoisted, the average grades of ore found, and the second-hand engines it purchased, all made it a typical nineteenth century Cornish metal mine.

Apart from its beautiful setting, the attraction of Killifreth , for industrial archaeologist and casual visitor alike, is its wealth of surface evidence of mining on the site. Visible remains span the whole period of recorded mining on the site, from the end of the medieval period to the 1920s, when the mine finally ceased production. Hawkes enginehouse and the tapering grace of its magnificent chimney, stand as a memorial to over five centuries of intermittant activity. Few pass along the road to Scorrier without a glance toward that silhouette. They cannot fail to be impressed by the permanence with which the past has stamped itself upon the landscape of the present.

EARLIEST TIMES

THE earliest period of the Cornish tin industry is shrouded in obscurity and vague traditions. Legends about Phoenician traders and Joseph of Arimathea, vie for position with attested historical fact, and somehow get intermixed. The written history seems to begin in the fourth century BC, when Pytheas, a Greek explorer and geographer, visited west Cornwall and described the tin trade there. Diodorus Siculus, a Roman historian who lived in the first century BC, apparently used the account by Pytheas, and described how the tin trade followed well-established trade routes across Gaul (modern day France) to the Mediterranean Sea, at Marseilles. The tin was then distributed by traders to ports throughout the eastern Mediterranean world. Thus, the legends that connect the inhabitants of Palestine with those historical first-century, middle eastern traders, appear to have some basis in fact, even if there is no evidence that Phoenicians themselves ever visited the coast of Cornwall. Archaeology has tended to push the antiquity of the Cornish tin trade even further back in time.(2)

Until the middle of the fifteenth century (c.1430-60) most Cornish tin was produced by streaming alluvial or eluvial deposits, but in some areas, where the cassiterite was seen in lodes at surface, mining was already widespread. In Gwennap and Kenwyn parishes for example, lode mining was well-established by the fourteenth century, and Killifreth probably saw underground mining in the late medieval period. Tinbounds are referred to in a will dated 1517. "Whelle Yeste in Kyllvrethe Downe" was a bounded tinwork owned by Thomas Tregian, and the context suggests the working was well-established by that date. (3)

Thereafter, there were continuous references to tin mining at Killifreth throughout the sixteenth century. A document dated 1523 refers to tin mined at Killifreth, "Crukebrace (Creegbrawse), Coysechace (?Chacewood) & Saveak (Saveock)." (4) Sixty-two years later, in 1585, Killifreth was still a significant tin producer, for it was stated: "The woodys of Kilyvregh muste be viewed I thinke … the tynn there must be consyderyd." (5) The tin lay at shallow depth throughout Killifreth Woods. Examination of Killifreth and Unity woods reveal the extent that the surface has been turned over in the search for tin, and the many workings, accessible until recently via a score of small, narrow shafts, shows how easily obtainable tin must have been at that time. Large cassiterite crystals were a feature of the workings there, and good specimens have been found there in recent years. During the medieval and Tudor periods the existence of rich tin deposits was often the cause of unscrupulous rogues invading tinworks and stealing the produce. Sometimes they would try to get possession of the whole property. This may have been a factor in the violence which occurred at Killifreth in the year 1517, when the occupier had to flee into the adjacent woods for her own safety. The perpetrators of this deed were Truro businessmen, led by one William Langhar and his brother, Stephen. Stephen was a Kenwyn constable, who was notorious for his violence. On another occasion he had stabbed to death a William Hoskin for refusing to leave a public house and assist him. In 1517, according to "Phelippa Carmynowe wydow … William Langhar of Truro, gentleman, Stephen Langhar of the same, gentleman, Thomas Tregian, merchant, and John Tregyan, merchaunte, assembled their servants and others with swerds naked redy drawen, went to Killyfregh, trusting to have found your oratrix (the widow) and her servants ther and then murdred them, but she had knowledg of their coming and departed, but is still in grett fere through their threats." (6)

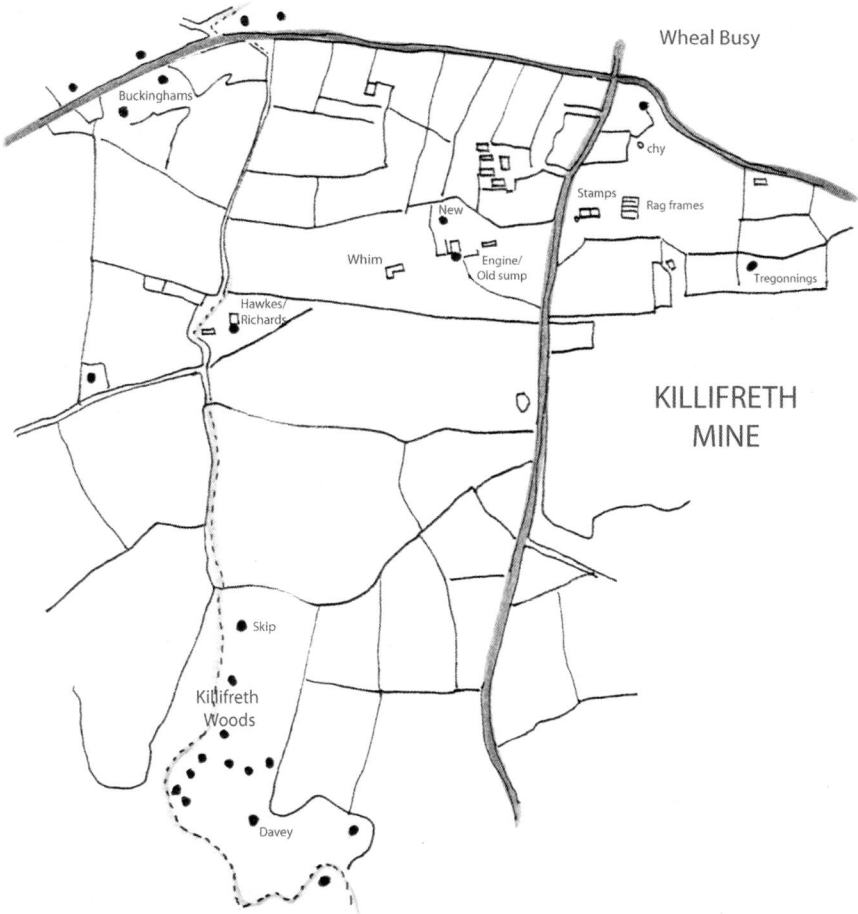

Map of Killifreth, based on one drawn by Eric Rabjohns of Carharrack.

SEVENTEENTH CENTURY

UNTIL the end of the seventeenth century the area between Kenwyn Parish boundary and the village of Chacewater was called Killifreth Downs. Killifreth included the woods on the west, and a large part of the country between the woods and Creegbrawse Mine, and the areas known as Salem, Wheal Busy and Wheal Daniel. The low moor land was bounded as stream works, which worked for alluvial tin, and the woods and downs as mine bounds. As has been noted above, Killifreth was worked for tin throughout the sixteenth century, but it was in the seventeenth century that the tin working records form a continuous series.

As well as lying close to the parish boundary, Killifreth also lay on the edge of Tywarnhaile (Tywarnhayle) Stannary District. The boundaries of stannary districts were not always precise, and Killifreth, like some of her neighbours, appears to have drifted between the jurisdiction of Penwith & Kerrier Stannary, based at Helston, and Tywarnhaile, based at Truro. Certainly, even Poldice, firmly within the stannary of Penwith & Kerrier, found it more convenient to take its tin to Truro for coinage, rather than the more distant Helston.

On November 24th 1615, the Harris family of Perranarworthal and St Clement, were involved in the sale of tinbounds called 'Pitte Cassane & Pitte Laworne in Kenwyn'. (7) These two small tinworks were on land that became known as Chacewater Bal. A 'bal' in Cornish mining was a group or district of tinbounds. Chacewater Bal later became famous as Wheal Busy. Two years later, Alexander and Humphry Daniall, Truro businessmen, held part shares in Higher, Middle and Lower 'Lowarne'.(8) In 1631, Humphry Buckingham, a fuller, of Kenwyn, owned shares in tinbounds including 'Pitse Cassowe'.(9) In 1639, several pairs of bounds on Killifreth Downs were referred to: "Wheel an Bucket, Greegbare, Wheel an Bush Vean, White worke by Kellyfryth lande and … 2 payrs of bounds … one at the East and the other West … Pit Kaser … weele Good Lucke … three payre in Kellyfreth lane and called out of dept (debt)." Altogether there were eleven pairs of tinbounds listed on Killifreth Downs. It is of interest that apart from the Harris family, who had a long association with mining at Chacewater, there is mention of the Buckingham and Daniell families, who have maintained connections with local mines until the twentieth century. (10)

A document dated 1676 lists many tinbounds on Killifreth Downs and woods, and makes mention of 'Mettle worke' as part of Chacewater Bal.(11) At about the same time, Richard Dyer, of Oxford University, listed a copper specimen from 'Metal Work at Kenwyn'.(12) Incidentally, Wheal Busy area was sometimes called 'Pitscassowe Downs' at that time. 'Wheale an Dayet by Pitslowarne Mills', 'Wheale an Frane by the wood side', 'Reseth Dew', 'Reseth South', Wheal Saturday' snd 'Wheale an Vor', were also there.

During the 1680s, with the increasing industrialisation of England, and the unfortunate loss of traditional copper suppliers, attention was drawn to waste material on Cornish tin mines, known as 'poder'. Alert agents of the Gloucestershire copper smelters, noted that this material contained copper ore. Men like Gabriel Wayne and John Costar quickly realised the potential of this source, and began buying up large tonnages, which lay around the surfaces of the tin mines. Relistian and Trevaskis in Gwinear, Dolcoath and the Roskears in Camborne, Pool and Penhellick in Illogan, Pedandrea and Sparnon in Redruth and Poldice and Tresavean in Gwennap, all discovered that beneath the shallow tin, often quite close to the surface, lay rich copper mineralisation. Wayne and Costar soon began buying shares in these mines.(13)

When Sir Clement Clarke, Talbot Clerke, Francis Scobell MP, Henry Vincent MP and the Carlyon family of Tregrehan, set up their copper smelting operation at Polrudden, near St Austell, in the 1690s, their agents visited Chacewater Bal to try to purchase the copper ore there for their smelter. The Boscawens, who were the mineral lords, refused the approach, and Costar and his associates secured the supply for their Bristol based company. From this period onward Cornish mining was dominated by copper production, and the wealth of the gentry, hitherto quite modest, began to grow at an enormous speed. However, the western part of these workings, at Killifreth itself, remained outside these changes for the most part, due to persistent tin mineralisation. To the east, Chacewater Bal's tin lodes contained large quantities of rich copper ore within a short distance of the surface. This area, by then being called Wheal Busy, soon eclipsed the small tin mines to the west. (14)

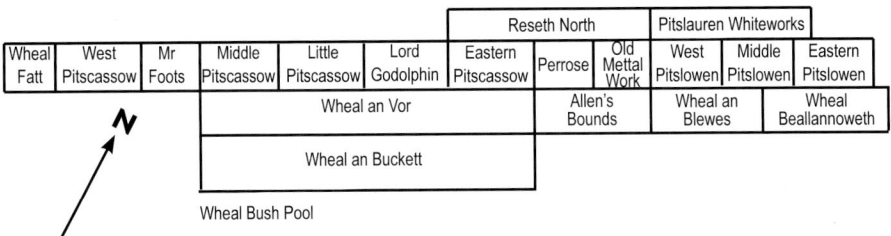

								Reseth North		Pitslauren Whiteworks	
Wheal Fatt	West Pitscassow	Mr Foots	Middle Pitscassow	Little Pitscassow	Lord Godolphin	Eastern Pitscassow	Perrose	Old Mettal Work	West Pitslowen	Middle Pitslowen	Eastern Pitslowen
	Wheal an Vor						Allen's Bounds		Wheal an Blewes		Wheal Beallannoweth
	Wheal an Buckett										
Wheal Bush Pool											

The relative positions of tin bounds on Chacewater Bal in the 17th Century. Identified from tin bound registrations dated between 1615 and 1676.

LOCATION, SIZE & NAMES

KILLIFRETH, like most Cornish mines, did not cover a specific, limited area. At different times it has worked different parts of the sett, sometimes being confined to the north-east corner, nearest to Wheal Busy, sometimes stretching past Hawkes Shaft to the west, and sometimes working only the northern part of Killifreth Woods. Occasionally, the owners have held the setts or bounds for the whole of what we now call Killifreth Mine. In 1929, E R Bawden wrote that Killifreth was bounded on the north by Great Wheal Busy, on the south by Wheal Unity Wood Mine, on the west by the Gwennap-Kenwyn parish boundary, and on the east by a line running through the western side of Chacewater. He commented that in 1828 the mine had been divided into setts or tinbounds known as Good Fortune, West Good Fortune, Lane, Wood, Wheal Fat Mine and Wheal Union Mine. A map of Killifreth Estate, dated September 1820, shows the north, north-east, south-east and south parts of the mine divided into tinbounds, and the central part, which comprised most of the woods, as either unworked or occupied by Wheal Union Mine. At that time the sett was worked by three separate mines: Wheal Fat, in the north-east corner, Wheal Union, in the centre, and Wood Mine at the southern end of the sett. A mine plan of Wheal Busy ('Chacewater Mine'), dated 1813, shows the north-eastern corner of Killifreth, between New Shaft and Buckingham's Stack, as Wheal Vor, and part of Chacewater Mine. (15)

Just as Killifreth has not always worked the same area, so it has not always been known by the same name. The earliest small mines on the property were known by their tinbound names, such as Wheal Good Fortune, Wheal Fat, Wheal Union and Wood Mine. Originally, a mine work (work=Cornish wheal) was often known by the name of the lode it worked, and vice versa. As groups of tinbounds were joined together, especially in the eighteenth century, so one of the bound names was used for the whole operation, or a different name was chosen. In the nineteenth century some mine names were merely the names of London-based companies, or names thought up to attract 'up country' investment. Many mines retained names which were purely local, and often associated with mining on the site for generations. In the late eighteenth and early nineteenth centuries, the wooded southern part of Killifreth, was known as Wheal Union, with Wood Mine at the southern extremity. It continued in the early decades of the nineteenth century with these names, but then became part of a large mine known as Wheal Unity Wood. Sometimes the combine went as far south as the boundary with Wheal Unity, and was known as North Wheal Unity. It was also known for a time as Wheal Unity Wood & Tolgullow United, and as West Poldice. (16)

The July 1772 cost book account for Wheal Unity shows an interest in Killifreth:

William Richards was paid by the mine to draw up "two written setts for Lady St Aubin & Mr Hunt, 1/6 each in Killifreth wood." The north-western part of the property, between Hawkes Shaft and Wheal Busy, was designated as 'Lane' and 'Good Fortune' tinbounds, although apart from the area known as Wheal Vor, there is little evidence of it being worked, other than, perhaps, by Chacewater Mine. A branch of the County Adit was driven into the north-west corner of Killifreth from Chacewater Mine, in the late eighteenth century. (17)

As a mine name, Killifreth does not appear to have been used until half way through the nineteenth century. The references to tin mining there in the sixteenth century, and the mention in 1772, are to the location. The first use of the name was probably in 1858, when the County Adit cost book lists the mine as an independent contributor toward maintenance. The name Killifreth was used once the mine was centred upon Engine ('Old Sump') Shaft and Richards (Hawkes or 'Flat Rod') shafts. (18)

GEOLOGY

THE country rock at Killifreth is sedimentary, of the Falmouth and Mylor series. This clay-slate is known locally as 'killas', and varies from extremely hard to quite soft. The killas overlays granite, which is about 1,200 feet (360m) from surface on the western side of the mine. Nearer to Carn Marth, granite is found at surface or at a shallow depth.

The property is traversed by several elvan (felspar porphyry) dykes, two important crosscourses (faults), and four main ore-bearing lodes or veins. The crosscourses intersect the lodes at right-angles, heaving them up to 12 feet (3.5m) off line. The minerals in these faults have no commercial value, although cobaltine has been found at adit level. The principal ore-bearing lodes are Main or North Lode, Wheal Vor, Middle and South lodes.

Main or North Lode is a caunter lode, which cuts across the usual strike of the lodes in the district. Its strike of 77 degrees north-west contrasts with the other lodes, which are approximately 77 degrees north-east. Like the other lodes at Killifreth it dips to the north. North Lode has been worked extensively from Hawkes Shaft, between adit and the 90fm level. Large quantities of good grade tin and copper ore have come from this lode, which seems to be especially rich where it is intersected by the main crosscourse and by Wheal Vor and South lodes.

Nearly all exploration and production on Middle Lode has been confined to the west of the main crosscourse, although it is believed to be rich as it goes eastward. This lode was also known as 'Grove Lode'. Middle Lode has been worked extensively to the 70fm level, and some exploration has taken place at the 90fm level, where a crosscut connects it to Hawkes Shaft. This lode was opened up from Hawkes Shaft, by means of south crosscuts at the 50, 70 and 90fm levels. Skip Shaft was deepened to the 70fm level on Middle Lode. The 40fm level has been driven to within 100 yards (90m) of the mine's western boundary, and the ground between adit and the 50fm level has been developed for a considerable distance westward. From about 200 yards (180m) west of the main crosscourse, Middle Lode carries appreciable quantities of wolfram. Small specimens of molybdenite have also been found in the lode.

Where Middle Lode has been disordered by greenstone it has separated into numerous stringers of pure cassiterite, leaving clear, barren ground between. The miners were enabled, by the softness of the cassiterite and the hardness of the host rock, to separate the ore underground, throwing the waste onto 'stulls'. These stulls were timber platforms

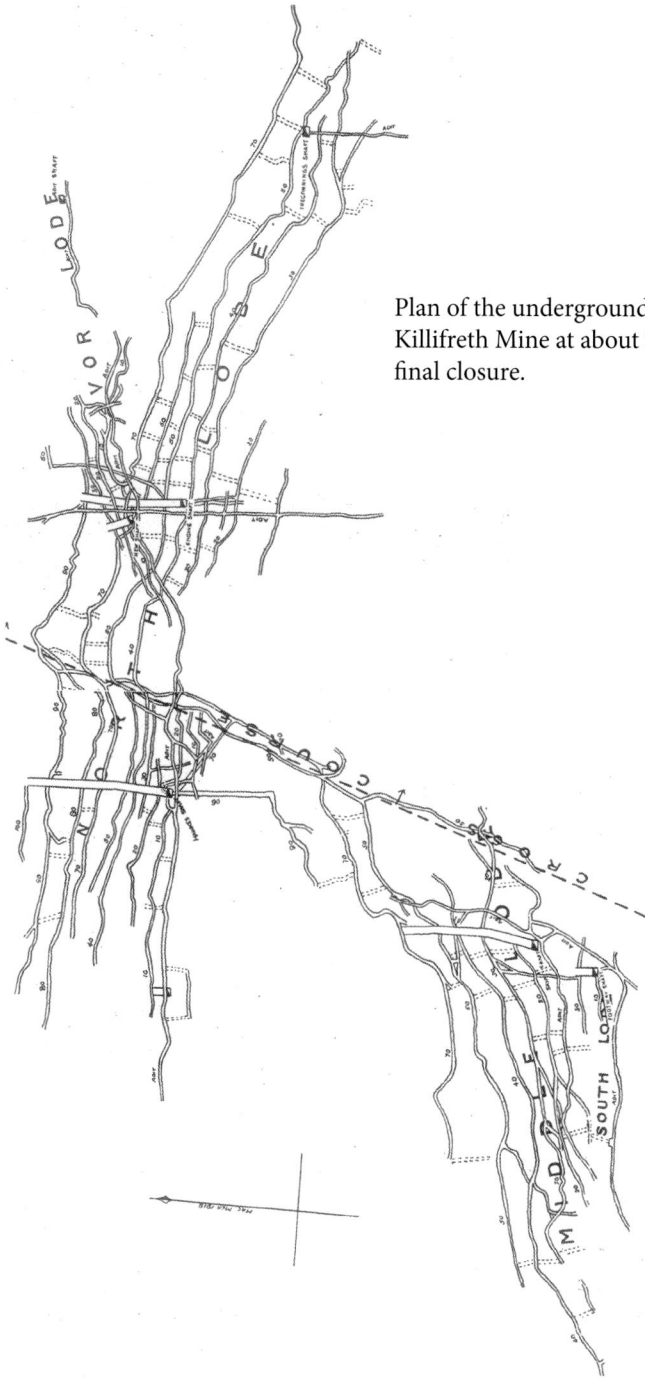

Plan of the underground workings of Killifreth Mine at about the time of its final closure.

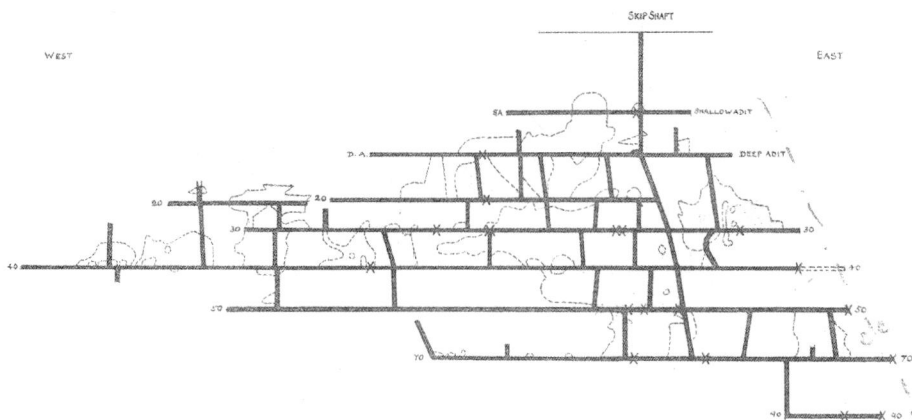

Long section of Middle Lode, one of the principal mineralised structures at Killifreth. Skip Shaft lies close to the northern edge of Killifreth Woods and was the main access shaft for the lode. From the 50 to the 90 fathoms levels Middle Lode was also worked from Hawkes Shaft. The section shows the workings at the time of the mine's closure.

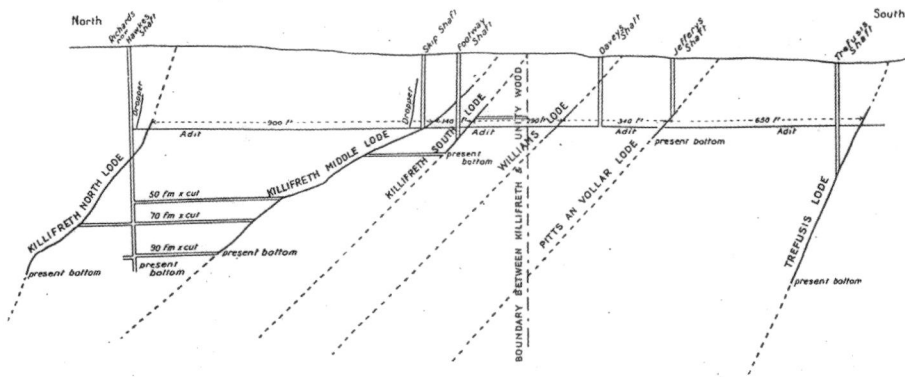

Transverse section of Killifreth Mine from roughly north to south. Hawkes (Richards) Shaft on the north of the sett through to Trefusis Shaft on the south side of Killifreth (Unity) Woods. The section shows the extent of the workings in the early 20th century.

resting on heavy timbers, which had been put in place to support the 'hanging wall'. The problems inherent in working such patchy tin ground was described by E R Bawden, thus:

"The lode in places has to be worked on the tribute system. One particular case may be cited as an illustration. Eight men were put stoping between the 30 and 40fm levels on contract, the average of the ore broken by them assaying 9lb SnO2, per ton, and no foot or hanging wall rock was mined. It was decided to let the stope on tribute to the men, paying a standard price of £85 per ton for black tin, and a tribute of 10s in the £, out of which the men paid the cost of materials. Under this system the ground produced from 2½ to 3 tons of black tin every four weeks; by any other system this particular stope could not be mined profitably. The tributers mined the waste first, leaving the richer portion standing, which was subsequently broken down very carefully on bags, which had been previously laid on the floor. Discontinuous as the lode undoubtedly is, these small patches occur with sufficient regularity to enable a fairly uniform grade of ore to be mined and milled."

Despite the patchy occurrence of cassiterite on Middle Lode, it proved well worth working. The lode varies in width from one to twelve feet (.3m to 3.5m), and carries values up to an incredible 50 percent black tin (cassiterite): 1,080 lb per ton! The average grade found on Middle Lode during the last periods of working was 39 lb per ton (1.75 percent), which is extremely good. Most of Killifreth's tin eventually came from Middle Lode.

At County Adit level, South Lode, also known as Wheal Union Lode, is about 46 yards (42m) south of Middle Lode. South Lode was worked in the early nineteenth century, mostly for copper ore, and very probably was stoped above and below the adit level in the eighteenth century. Where exposed the lode is between four and six feet wide (1.3m and 1.8m), and although mostly low grade (between 5 and 14 lb per ton), it was very easy to work and probably profitable at a shallow level. No serious attempts were made to develop the lode at depth: no crosscuts were driven into it and no sinking on it below the 30fm level.

Trefusis Lode was worked at the extreme southern end of the sett, particularly under Wood Mine and Unity Wood Mine. At County Adit level the lode was opened up for a distance of over 2,000 feet (600m). Its strike is east 30 degrees north and it underlies 20 degrees to the north-west. It was opened up from Broads, Symons and Magor shafts. It appears only to have been worked to any depth at Wheal Bush (between Magor and Broads shafts). The lode carried quantities of tin, copper and arsenic. (19)

THE NINETEENTH CENTURY MINE

At the beginning of the nineteenth century Cornish mining was just recovering from a period of slump. Abandoned mines were being reopened and new mines projected. Killifreth Woods were being worked by two separate mines, with Wheal Union to the north and North Wheal Unity to the south. Wheal Busy had developed Wheal Vor Lode into the north-east corner of Killifreth, by the crossroads. The earliest extant County Adit cost book has Wheal Union paying maintenance, for the year 1806, of 1/66th of the total cost. North Wheal Unity seems to have been operated by the management of Wheal Unity & Poldice, as a joint enterprise. (20)

In his *Report on a Survey of the Mining District of Cornwall from Camborne to Chacewater* (1819), Richard Thomas described Wheal Union as being in killas, drained by the 'Great (County) Adit', and worked no deeper than adit level, 258 feet (77m) below the surface. He wrote that Wheal Union had become amalgamated with North Wheal Unity Mine, and the County Adit cost book shows them under the title Wood Mine. Thomas described two main lodes at Wheal Union, the southern lode he called Wheal Union Lode, and the northern one he gives as Grove Lode. Grove Lode appears to be Killifreth's Middle Lode, and Wheal Union Lode would be Killifreth's South Lode. Their positions shown on Thomas' map, together with the descriptions of these lodes, seem to confirm this. (21)

The County Adit was driven into Wheal Union from Wheal Unity, via North Wheal Unity, by the 1790s. Thomas' map shows it entering the woods at Trefusis Shaft, and then extending to the northern edge of the woods. A branch, which starts just north of Davys Shaft, goes west. Another long branch was driven eastwards from Trefusis toward Zion Chapel, on Cox Hill. At that time the only connection to what became Hawkes Shaft section of Killifreth Mine, was the one from Wheal Busy, along Wheal Vor Lode. This branch went under the main road, and the one to Todpool, stopping near East Shaft. During the 1840s, a long crosscut extended the adit from Symons Shaft north to New Shaft and Engine Shaft. Thereafter it was pushed westward past Richards (Hawkes) Shaft, first on Wheal Vor Lode and then on North Lode. Concerning the crosscut north from Symons (Sandoes) Shaft, Michell makes some interesting points, in his July 1851 Letter Book. Under the heading of Wheal Unity Wood, he wrote: "In this mine they are still extending their crosscut north by 3 men and 4 boys which has now been extended nearly 300 fms north of Sandoes Shaft without any communication north of the shaft. The end is ventilated by virtue of Air Sollars and the stuff discharges by wagons on a Rail Road." The ability to ventilate the end by only using floor sollars is remarkable. The air needed to be carried 1,800 feet (540m) from the nearest shaft to the

Killifreth and the surrounding mines. The map drawn by Richard Thomas in 1819, was of the Camborne-Chasewater Mining District. The route of the County Adit ('The Great Adit') is shown as are the main lodes worked locally.

end, and then back beneath the wooden floor sollar, to keep the air in the end moving. The 'boys' moving the broken rock back to the shaft for hoisting had their tasks made easier by the use of wagons on track. (22)

For the rest of the century Killifreth was drained by means of the main branch of Country Adit through Wheal Unity and Poldice. During the early twentieth century it is probable that the connection via Wheal Vor Lode, at Wheal Busy, was extended, because maintenance records from the 1920s indicate that Killifreth and Wheal Busy used the direct route to the portal, through Creegbrawse. (23)

Between 1809 and 1823 considerable quantities of tin were mined in the shallow workings in Killifreth Woods, and Lord Falmouth benefited to the tune of £2,609 on an output of £42,411. By 1823 tin production had tailed off, to be replaced by significant tonnages of copper ore, being produced by Wood Mine. In the years 1823-53 there was £123,360 worth of copper ore sold by Wood Mine. (24)

Dines states that Killifreth was worked between 1826 and 1860 for copper, although the northern part of the sett does not seem to have been active. Little historical data has survived for the first half of the nineteenth century, and J Y Watson, writing in 1843, makes no mention of Killifreth. He does describe Unity Wood Tin & Copper Mine, however, and comments that although in the past it had yielded vast profits, it was at that time worked in a very desultory way, despite still employing 200 workers. In the years 1838 to 1842, it produced 6,307 tons of copper ore, worth £49,051. As with many mines in the eighteenth and nineteenth centuries, one part of the sett was working whilst the other part was idle, and the period between the years 1840 and 1860 was characterised by much change and uncertainty. (25)

By the end of the 1840s moves were afoot to develop the northern section of Killifreth. The County Adit was being extended northward from Symons Shaft, and according to a report by Captain Charles Thomas of Dolcoath Mine, it had intersected no less than sixteen lodes and branches. Although the rest of Thomas' report was not an encouraging one, he did concede that two or three of the lodes cut were probably worth working. (Captain Charles Thomas Letter to Messrs Hodge & Hockin June 2nd 1854) Captain Theophilus Michell of Chacewater, the Tregothnan mineral agent, took issue with Thomas over his conclusions, painting a much more sanguine picture of Killifreth's prospects. (Theo. Michell Letter to D Gunn at Tregothnan. June 10th 1854) Those investigations took place in 1854, and three years later a lease was granted to work the northern part of the sett, together with the wooded area. Under the 1857 lease, Richard Shaft was started, and it was intended to put a large pumping engine on it. Captain Joel Higgins was appointed mine manager, but although it started well, lack of capital soon created problems. By 1862 the mine was almost at a standstill. Sufficient had been done, however, for Killifreth's potential to be seen, and in 1864 a new cost book company was organised to exploit what had been discovered. By

Copy.

Dolcoath Mine, Camborne
2nd June 1854

Mess.rs Hodge & Hockin
    Gentlemen,

I have today gone over the estate of Killifreath, Kenwyn, agreeably to your instructions; — examining carefully its mineral characteristics and obtained what information I could relative to it from Capt.n Michell and now beg to send you the following report

This piece of ground is nearly surrounded with Mines, some of which continue to be highly productive and others, now idle, were so formerly except however Wht Unity Wood in the South West part worked as I am informed to the depth of 80 fms below the adit little has been done here below the adit level. From Wheal Unity Wood the dues paid to the Lord since 1810, as I find by extracts from the Books have been £8224.3.7 — From partial operations in other parts of the estate £351.4.6 Wheal Busy lying to the North East of and adjoining the estate paid dues during the same period to the amount of £17,148.1.6. Wheal Busy Lode passes through part of this ground towards the North West but has not been explored there, I believe, much below the adit level. The lode under will at no great depth pass out of the Estate but will be found probably of some value before it reaches that depth. The whole of the Estate at the surface is in clay slate, traversed by Elvan Courses.— Granite is found at the South West, in which Wheal Gorland and Wheal Unity formerly very productive, are found. This Granite dips East-

Letter, dated June 2nd 1854, from Capt. Charles Thomas, manager of Dolcoath, to Hodge & Hockin, agents of the Tregothnan Estate. Thomas had been asked to comment on the prospects of Killifreth Mine, and his report was not as optimistic as the mine management had hoped. Private Collection.

Chacewater 10th June 1854

Sir,
Killifreath Estate Kenwyn.

I have this day received the Copy of Capt Charles Thomas's Report of this property which I find is open to remark and as the subject is of some importance it ought not to be passed over in silence.

1st I cannot come to the same conclusion as Capt T. does relative to the Lode 50 fms short of the Cross cut which he says is the most important in appearance, as the Tin Lode about 50 fms south of this is a large well defined lode, and will probably yield more mineral than the other which Capt T has calculated on, but very little has been done to develope it. Between these two Lodes there is another which may prove equally Productive and which can be worked by the same machinery, and about 24 fms to the north there is another which has been opened on about 8 feet and which contains Copper Ore may be equally productive, and 26 fms still further north there is another Lode Capt T has made no remark on either of these three Lodes that can all be worked by the same machinery. Should these four Lodes prove so productive as the one calculated on by Capt T, the Dues would then amount to £42,000 by no means an improbable case, but looking at the district an highly probable one, yet as the ground is unexplored I would not value it so high, still the position and probability should be placed before you

2ndly I cannot come to the conclusion that Capt Thomas does that there will not be much Tin found in this locality— His words are "I see no reason to expect any considerable amount of Tin from that locality." The facts are directly opposed to this

Letter, dated June 10th 1854, from Capt. Theophilus Michell of Chacewater, Lord Falmouth's mineral agent, to D Gunn at Tregothnan, refuting the unflattering report of Capt. Thomas. Private Collection.

that time the County Adit had been driven to North and Wheal Vor lodes, and then westward past Richards Shaft. Engine and Richards shafts had been sunk on lode and had found good ore values, and the surface area was being organised to work efficiently and economically. Thomas Spargo's description of the mine, in 1865, shows that the new company brought together a new management team with enough backing capital to work profitably. (26)

"Killifreth, in Kenwyn, in 1,000 shares. Purser, Mr Edward Hawke Jun., Tregullow. Manager, Captain John Tremayne, Wheal Rose Scorrier. Lord, Viscount Falmouth. Dues 1-20th. Depth of adit, 43 fathoms. Depth under it, 30 fathoms. 30 men employed. Pumping-engine, 12-inch (rotary). Rocks, clay-slate and elvan. No returns in 1864.

The company have recently resumed the works, which were suspended a year or two. They are sinking the engine-shaft, which will intersect the lode at about 70 fathoms. There are numerous lodes in the sett, which appears to warrant extensive exploration. Great Wheal Busy lies contiguous to the mine, at the east, and Wheal Unity Wood, formerly rich, at the west." (27)

The new company continued work at Killifreth until 1896, when it was converted into a limited liability company. Several times during those 33 years the mine almost succumbed to the crises which beset Cornish mining generally, but it always recovered and soldiered on. Between 1870 and 1874 there was a sudden boom in mining, followed by an unexpected slump. In 1872, old, long-abandoned mines were reopening, and new ones, funded by 'up-country' cash, were also starting. The value of some mine shares went through the roof. This was followed by an almost total collapse of the tin price. Everywhere mines closed, most of them never to reopen. These vicissitudes saw Killifreth move from the doldrums in 1870, to top gear by 1872, and almost stopped by the end of 1874, when her tin revenue was halved. (28)

In 1872 Edward Hawke was replaced as purser by John Tregonning, and together with a variety of mine captains they introduced new plant to the mine. In 1873 Killifreth purchased a 50-inch Cornish beam engine to pump from Engine Shaft. It was bought from Wheal Daniell, half-a-mile to the east and cost £1,300, including an eleven ton boiler. This was all paid for by the recent high profits. The 50-inch had been installed at Wheal Daniell in the autumn of 1871, and had done very little work there. It was already second-hand when Wheal Daniell bought it. The pitwork for Engine Shaft came from Wheal Millett, in Crowan Parish. In 1872 William Buckingham became a mine captain at Killifreth, and a shaft, being sunk by the main road to the north of Hawkes Shaft, was named after him. He was also involved in building a chimney stack near the dressing floors, and this is still known by his name. In 1876 a 32-inch stamps engine was purchased for £560, the cost including buddles, two 16 head stamps axles and other dressing plant. The boiler house lay behind the enginehouse, and was large enough for two Cornish boilers. Until the end of the 1880s the 32-inch was adequate

Division of Cost below Separation 1858

Mine				
Consolidated Mines	270	6	10	4
United Mines	1106	26	16	7
St Day United Mines	689	16	14	3
Wheal Jewell	25	.	12	2
Wheal Damzel	100	2	8	5
Wheal Fork Consols	25	.	12	2
Killifreth	49	1	3	6
St Michael Penkevil & Greenbrawse	25	.	12	2
Wheal Clifford	100	2	8	6
Wheal Andrew	196	4	15	0
North Damzel	25	.	12	2
South Gorland	25	.	12	2
Carharrack Mine	25	.	12	2
Wheal Henry	25	.	12	2
Gt Wheal Busy	324	7	17	8
Nangiles	25	.	12	2
Romance	25	.	12	2
South Clinton Holt Edgcumbe	25	.	12	2
North Treskerby	25	.	12	2
	3109			
		£75	8	0

1858 extract from the County Adit Cost Books, which shows the earliest reference to Killifreth as a separate mine, paying toward the adit's maintenance. Private Collection.

for the tonnage stamped, but eventually the engine had a 36-inch cylinder fitted, and another 32 stamps heads erected. (29)

In 1879 Captain John Michell joined the mine as mine captain, and the following year he replaced George Tremayne as manager. Killifreth, like other tin mines, was just getting back into full production in 1880. The next decade had its share of problems, but the mine experienced a fairly long period of expansion. North and Wheal Vor lodes were developed and stoped, Old Sump (Engine Shaft) and Hawkes Shaft were deepened, and crosscuts at the 50 and 70fm levels were pushed south from Hawkes Shaft to Middle Lode. As this lode flattens as it dips north, Hawkes becomes closer as it gets deeper. In 1891 Captain Joe Tamblyn joined the mine. He was a very energetic miner, who had worked in Italy, Wisconsin and South Africa before arriving at Killifreth. He stayed there until 1887, when he went to Basset Mines. Thereafter he was a mine captain at South Wheal Crofty (1892-95), Dolcoath (1895-1903), Spain (1903-06), East Pool (1906-08) and Condurrow (1908-10), where he became manager. The *Mining Journal* described him as an agent of considerable energy and skill. Tamblyn was replaced at Killifreth in 1887 by Captain Oliver Northey, whose family had a long association with mines on the County Adit. (30)

The letter books of James Bryant, mineral agent at Tregothnan, give a lot of information on the working of Killifreth Mine during the 1880s. Two letters, dated July and November 1880, indicate the recent near-closure of the mine. The first concerns an application from Captain Michell, the manager, to explore Tin Lode at shallow level from Footway Shaft, Wheal Busy. Wheal Busy had been closed since 1866, despite an expensive attempt to restart it in 1872, when the water had been pumped to the 50fm level. Bryant gave permission to carry out this exploration, although we are not told the results. (31)

The other letter, dated November 29th 1880, is also very interesting. The Purser, Tregonning, forwarded a complaint about the height of the shears at Hawkes Shaft. Apparently, the shears could be seen through a gap in the trees from Tregullow House, the home of the Hawke family, after whom the shaft had been renamed in 1864. Edward Hawke had been purser at the mine when it reopened, and Richards Shaft had been renamed in his honour. Bryant investigated the complaint and found that when Richards Shaft had originally been sunk, in 1857, it had been an engine shaft. It was reasonably pointed out that if the shaft had had a large engine on it, as had been intended, then the inhabitants of Tregullow would have had a lot more to see than a mere nine feet (2.8m) of shears through the trees. Bryant's letter mentions that the shears were 42 feet (13m) high, and that Hawkes was being pumped at that time by means of flat rods from Engine (Old Sump) Shaft. Hawkes was also referred to as Flat Rod Shaft in the letter. (32)

In April 1884, Tregonning acted for the mine in trying to get a reduction in the dues.

KILLIFRETH MINE,

11TH FEBRUARY, 1881.

To the Shareholders.

GENTLEMEN,

WESTERN GROUND.

Hawkes, or the Flat Rod Shaft, is now 7 fathoms below the 10 fathom level, and in the last 2 or 3 feet sunk the Copper Lode and Caunter Lode have been intersected in the south west corner of the Shaft, and an unusually large quantity of water is issuing therefrom; the ground above is drained in consequence for 150 fathoms in length—we consider this to be a very favorable indication, and from the little that has been seen of the lodes in the bottom of the Shaft, we have every reason to expect that they will be productive for Mineral. This extraordinary increase of water has necessitated the changing of the present 8 inches lift to 10 inches, which is now being done, and will, we expect, be completed about a week hence, when the sinking will be resumed.

The Lode in the 10 fathom level west of Hawke's Shaft is about 18 inches wide and of a promising nature. This will form a junction with the Copper Lode about 15 or 20 fathoms west of the present end, and from the appearances of these lodes, at the adit, west of the junction, we have reason to expect satisfactory returns.

In consequence of the water being let down at Hawke's, the New Shaft, 90 fathoms west of Hawke's and 17 fathoms above, on the course of the lode, has been entirely drained, and sinking here has been commenced below the Adit level, where the lode is from 4 to 5 feet wide, of a most promising nature, and producing good saving work for Tin.

The lode in the Adit end west, which is extended 40 fathoms west of the New Shaft, has greatly improved, in the last 6 feet driven, and it is now worth £5 per fathom for Tin with every appearance of becoming still more valuable.

We are also driving a shallow adit west from New Shaft, where the lode is also presenting a much better appearance; it is about 4 feet wide and worth £7 per fathom for Tin.

OLD SUMP SHAFT.

We expect the rise from the 40 to the 30 fathom level will be holed in a few days, when the driving of 40 fathom level east will be resumed.

The lode in the 30 fathom level east has been, and still is producing, occasionally, good stones of Copper Ore, and the appearance justify the hope that there is mineral ground before us in this direction.

It will be seen, from the above, that the workings are opening up favourably, and we are pleased to find ourselves in the position to state that the prospects, generally, are more cheering than they have been during the last 2 years or more.

We have raised about 1½ tons of Tin, which is not returned, in consequence of a mishap to the Flues, at the Burning House, caused by the late severe frost, but £75 will be credited to day, on account of this Tin.

We are. Gentlemen,

Your obedient Servants,

JOHN MICHELL, Manager.

JOSEPH PAULL, Agent.

Report to Killifreth 's adventurers by the manager, Capt. John Michell and mine captain, Joseph Paull, dated February 11th 1881. Note, Hawkes (Flat Rod) Shaft was only 17 fathoms below the Deep Adit level.

Times were hard and the mine was struggling again. Bryant had passed on the request to Lord Falmouth, who had apparently replied that times were hard for everyone – peers of the realm included! Afterwards, Tregonning met Bryant in the street at Truro and pressed him for a favourable hearing. When told of his lordship's reply, he requested that Bryant at least not push the mine too hard for the £210 already owing. (33)

Throughout the 1880s Bryant's letters were peppered with references to Killifreth, although most were to do with him going underground to inspect the workings for the estate, or the sales of tin and the consequent dues owing. What the references do show, is that unlike the vast majority of mines in the area, Killifreth was alive and well. During the last quarter of the nineteenth century Killifreth was the most consistently active mine on the County Adit. (34)

It was during the 1880s that Killifreth moved, albeit very briefly, into the list of top tin producers in Cornwall. In the years 1884-88 the mine averaged 151 tons of black tin a year. This put it in 22nd place among Cornish tin producers. To put these figures into perspective, during those years Dolcoath, which was at the top of the list throughout, averaged 2,484 tons of black tin *per annum*. South Wheal Crofty only managed an average of 122 tons during those years.

In 1884 Robert Symon's *Gazetteer of Cornwall,* described Killifreth thus: "Killifreth, Kenwyn, a tin mine near Scorrier, land of Lord Falmouth. Good prospects. Tin ore sold in 1882, £12,273; ditto 'whits', £2,255; copper £29." Whits or whitts were crushed ore not yet dressed. Symon's also listed Killifreth among those mines that had paid dividends, and added that the mine was held in 6,000 shares. (35)

By the end of the 1880s, Killifreth was having to face problems due to its success. The extensive stoping of North and Wheal Vor lodes, together with developments on Middle Lode, meant that increased water was flowing into the mine. The old 50-inch engine could no longer cope, especially as the mine was by then 600 feet (180m) below adit level. In 1891, it was decided to supplement the 50-inch engine with a larger one at Hawkes Shaft. An 80-inch engine was purchased from North Treskerby for £575. The price included balance bob, all main rods, a whim, capstan, wire rope and all the gear to go with it. With so many mines closing the prices of second-hand engines was very low, to Killifreth's advantage. The 80-inch engine had been built in 1860 for Wheal Falmouth & Sperries (Kea), and had been purchased by Lanyons of Redruth, in 1869. Lanyons had a flourishing second-hand engine business. In 1872, they sold the engine to North Treskerby, who used it on Doctors Shaft. They paid £800 for the engine and £250 for the boilers. Once Hawkes Shaft was sunk vertically to the 100fm level and all the timber sets and pitwork was installed, the 80-inch soon got on top of the water problem. (36)

Disaster continued to stalk the ailing Cornish mining industry during the 1890s, due mainly to extremely low tin prices, high pumping costs and an acute shortage of skilled labour. Letters and reports from the period show that mines were often desperate for labour. Australia, America and South Africa were taking thousands of Cornish miners, and India, South America, Mexico and other regions were also helping to make miners scarce in Cornwall.

In 1891 another problem also reared its ugly head. Due to bad feeling on the part of many miners still in Cornwall, there was a spate of vandalism. Dolcoath and Killifreth had their pitwork damaged; at East Pool a dam sealing off old, flooded workings was damaged; at the Wheal Frances and Basset mines there was a series of fires, as there had been at Dolcoath. These acts may have resulted from the greedy attitude of some of the owners, from militant trade unionism, or from mines applying new work practices, due to incipient government legislation. One group, frequently seen at the time as the principal perpetrators of these acts, was made up of miners returning from America and other areas, where militancy was more widespread. (37)

During the period when Hawkes new engine was being erected, Killifreth gained a new junior mine captain, R A James. He was no ordinary miner. As a boy he had gone underground with his father, an old tributer. When he was old enough, instead of continuing mining, he had been sent to work in a foundry at Hayle, where he stayed for three years. In 1879 he went to America, living in some of the roughest mining camps in Colorado. He worked in mills on large mines, and worked as a miner in small ones. At one time he leased the North Star Gold & Silver Mine, next to the famous Yankee Girl Mine, at Silverton, South Colorado. He turned a poor mine into a rich one, and despite paying over half his gains in royalties, still made a lot of cash. On one occasion he and four others were travelling through a lawless district when their stagecoach was held up at gun-point by masked gangsters. After pillaging the mail for valuables, the robbers left the miners alone, and bade them a courteous 'Good night'. James trecked in snow shoes over 13,000 foot high passes in the Rocky Mountains, lived for months in tiny log cabins and mined in appalling conditions. Eventually, with a pocket full of gold, he returned to his native Cornwall. He then became a mine adventurer, before returning to the practical side of mining as a mine captain. Captain John Michell liked James' pragmatic and logical approach to mining, and together they set about re-modernising Killifreth, as Michell, Tregonning and Tamblyn had done a decade earlier. (38)

In 1892, Tregonning died afer twenty years as purser. He was replaced by Thomas Trounson, who was to stay at Killifreth until it closed. When John Michell died, in 1893, James was appointed manager, and continued to implement what they had planned together. If anything, James moved faster and further than Michell would have done. A 22-inch whim engine was erected between Hawkes and Engine shafts, able to hoist from either shaft. The cylinder of the 32-inch stamps engine was replaced by a 36-inch, and the number of stamps heads was doubled to 64. Skip Shaft, on the northern edge of the woods, was deepened on Middle Lode, and connections between Hawkes and the south part of the sett were improved. James introduced innovations at Killifreth that were ahead of the times. Shift bosses were introduced underground, in line with his belief in the American system of more complete supervision underground. Tributing was expanded, as he believed it gave miners more incentive and made them more efficient in breaking certain sorts of lode. He introduced drilling machines into development ends, and more rapidly opened up new ground. James brought to Killifreth the first double-decked 'Yankee safety cage' to be used in Cornwall. It was designed and built by Sara's foundry at Tolgus, Redruth, to James' specifications. It had catches, which gripped the sides of the runners in the event of the wire rope breaking. In 1894 the pinions of the whim engine broke, causing the rope to snap. Instead of being precipitated to the bottom of the shaft, the catches held, and the cage stopped safely. The cage was used for man-riding and for hoisting trams of ore up the shaft. Captain James is best remembered for his 'big is beautiful' philosophy of mining. He thought that mines should be operated on the principle of the greater the tonnage, the less the cost per ton. He was an extremely strong advocate of converting the mine into a limited liability company. (39)

Much has been written in the *Mining Journal*, the *West Briton* and by J H Collins, about the effects of the conversion upon Killifreth. Once things began to go wrong, shortly after the creation of the limited company, all the wise men of mining tutted and criticised. The October 23rd 1897 *Mining Journal* referred to this 'warning against crude and ill-considered schemes', and wrote that things had gone 'sadly wrong since the change to Limited Liability' at Killifreth. Collins added, in 1912, that the new company, "launched into expensive schemes of development without previously securing a working capital, with the result that the mine was abandoned in a sort of panic." (40)

Almost everything said in 1897, about the closure, shows that it was the company and not the mine that was suspect. Despite criticism of Captain James for everything from the state of the pitwork to the installation of 'Yankee machines', it appears that the fault lay with the times and not the man. With a higher price for tin, more skilled labour available, and the luck all mining enterprises need, Killifreth may well have fulfilled its promise. Captain James was an aggressive and opinionated man, who made enemies as frequently as he converted backers to his view. He answered critics of the pitwork, by pointing out that he had not in fact purchased it, but only supervised its installation. On the 'Yankee machine' (safety cage) he pointed out that it had worked efficiently, and proved safe when a breakage occurred. His arguments on the economy of working low-grade ore by reducing costs per ton are still widely accepted. (41)

Whatever the truth about the reasons for closure, by autumn 1897, the shareholders (and creditors) had had enough. Local parties, some of whom had a good knowledge of the lode at Killifreth, offered to finance new exploration in specific areas. Crosscuts from Tregonnings Shaft, to intersect Middle Lode, and from Skip Shaft to South Lode, were among the favourite suggestions. (42) But, it was all in vain. Between 1891 and

1896 tin revenue had been very healthy, peaking, in 1893 at £17,617, but by the summer of 1897 production was reduced by a third, and the mine had looked extremely shaky. In the September 25th 1897 *Mining Journal*, the plant was advertised for sale by the liquidator, Thomas Trounson. The 80-inch and 50-inch pumping engines, the 36-inch stamps engine, with 64 heads of stamps, the 22-inch whim engine, the 12-inch capstan engine, and all the rest of the mining, crushing and dressing gear were up for tender. (43) The November 27th 1897 *Mining Journal* reported that the liquidator had sold the mine to W J Trythal of Carnon Chemical Works, Redruth. By then, the mine was preparing for a new career as a training mine, and Truro Mining School had taken it over by the end of the year. (44)

Mining did not stop at Killifreth, however, for 'tributers' moved into stopes above the adit level, and production continued on a very limited scale. These tributers were also known as 'free setters', and they worked without official permission. As at Poldice, Wheal Daniell, Wheal Busy, Wheal Uny and many other abandoned tin mines in the depressed mining regions of Cornwall, such informal mining became a mainstay of the local economy. Tregothnan, like many other estates, did not altogether approve of this practice, and sometimes withheld permission when it was sought, or actively strove to stop it. After the 1880 *Employers Liability Act*, Lord Falmouth's agent had anxiously enquired as to where the estate stood when unofficial mining was taking place in its mines. Where the practice continued regardless, Falmouth's agent exacted some dues by locating the miners through the tin streamers who bought their tin. Bryant's letters contain references to the need to locate these small buyers of black tin, which was sometimes dressed in clandestine operations, so that the mineral lord could obtain some dues. During the 1920s and 1930s many local mines were operated by such groups of men. One operation at Wheal Uny, Redruth, was only halted when the noise of blasting and tramming got too much for the farmer, whose kitchen was less than fifty feet (15m) above the main stope. (45)

Killifreth Mine.   15/3/99.

Sales from 1858 to 1871   £ 2705 – 9 – 1
From 1871 to 17/2/91   11649 . 5 . 4
    17/2/91 to 21/1/96   77367 – 5 – 11
Year 1896.   –   5918 – 11. 3
    do.   (Limited)   4171 – 6 – 6
    1897   (do.)   5292 – 12.8
    1898.   (In Hand)   808 . 4 – 6
                                          £. 207.912 – 15. 3

Sales from 1858 to 1871. "Copper"   £ . 2346 . 2 . 8
                          "Tin"   359 . 6 . 5
do.   1871 to 1898 "Tin." – £ 199638 . 19 . 7
                   "Copper" –   2655 . 16 . 11
                   "Arsenic" –   2893 – 12 . 6
                   "Mundic" –   13 . 17 . 2
                   "Ochre"   –   5 – 0 . 0
                                  £. 205207 . 6 . 2
Brot. down sales from 1858 to 1871. –   2705 . 0 . 1
                                  £ 207.912 . 15 . 3

Summary of tin, copper, arsenic, mundic and ochre production between the years 1858 and 1898. It was prepared following the 1898 closure of the mine, and is dated March 15 1899. Private Collection.

Hawkes (Richards) pumping enginehouse in the 1890s. Th engine had an 80inch diameter cylinder. Note, the lower stack height prior to raising to improve the draught for the 85inch engine installed in 1913. The balance box is in the left foreground. Note also, the high-level tramway and wagon, and the sheave and capstan wheels.

The lower section of the dressing floors with the rag (rack) frames for slimes in the foreground. The concentrate went from these to the calciner and thence to the buddIes and tin yard kieves. The produce was 65-70 percent tin. In the background are the Old Sump and stamps enginehouses. The picture was taken in the 1890s.

The stamps. enginehouse in the 1890s. There were 64 heads of stamps (32 on each side). Note, the gantry for lifting the stamps heads. The engine had been a 32inch until 1893, when it was re-cylindered to 36inch diameter.

Two convex buddles at the tin yard. Note, the launder carrying water over the buddles into the tin yard. Picture taken in the 1890s.

Old Sump (Engine Shaft) pumping enginehouse. The engine had a 50inch cylinder and was erected in 1873, having been brought second-hand from Wheal Daniell. Picture taken in 1890s.

Early 20th century picture of a group of Killifreth workers beside an air receiver for a compressor. The two men on the left appear to be miners and one has a day's supply of dips (candles).

Magnificent 1913 photograph of Hawkes enginehouse (with stack smoking), the 22inch whim enginehouse (erected in 1892) and Old Sump enginehouse on the right. Note, the cable stand to carry the whim ropes from the winder to Old Sump.

Hawkes Shaft in the early 1920s. The winder house is on the left of the picture. It contained a horizontal steam engine.

Hawkes Shaft after the final closure of Killifreth. The eastern end of the winder house can be seen, with the boiler house between it and the enginehouse.

The double deck safety cage ('Yankee machine') designed by Capt. R A James and constructed by Sara's Foundry, Redruth in 1893/4. It was used for hoisting men and ore. In 1894, when the pinion of the hoisting engine broke, the wire rope snapped and the catches gripped the runners as they were designed to do. The cage stopped without damage being done. Dolcoath adopted one later and Geevor used one of similar design until its final closure in 1990.

THE FINAL WORKING

ONCE the opening decade of the twentieth century was passed, investors once again began to put money into reopening mines, which had closed in the black days of the 1890s. During 1911, plans were made to work Killifreth on a large scale. By 1912, work was progressing well, with shafts repaired, the County Adit checked and refurbished, crushing and dressing plant reorganised and another engine planned for Hawkes Shaft. A second-hand Perran Foundry engine was purchased from Wales, with an 85-inch cylinder. To give the fire a better draught the brickwork on the enginehouse chimney was doubled in height. The slender shape which has been a landmark ever since was the result, although from a purely practical standpoint, it is doubtful if it improved the draught very much, at least that was the opinion of Jack Trounson. Hawkes Shaft was refurbished, with work done to renew timbers and pitwork, and make good the connection at adit level. The shaft measures twelve feet by six feet six inches, and is vertical to 100 fathoms below the County Adit level. Before 1891 it had been an underlay shaft from the 20fm level, where it met the lode. It had then been equipped with an 18-inch diameter Cornish pump, which had used bucket lift from the 70fm level. The 85-inch engine had a ten foot stroke in the cylinder and a nine foot stroke outside. It raised 800 gallons a minute with ease, which was well over double the normal volume entering the mine. Built in 1871, it had spent 40 years in Welsh lead mines, where it allegedly pumped at up to 14 strokes a minute. Some claimed this was a world record for an engine of its size. When working at 14 strokes, at Great Fron Fownog, Mold, this 500 horse-power engine had pumped an incredible 1,333 gallons a minute. It had been thought, that South Crofty's Robinsons 80-inch held this distinction, when it is said to have pumped at 13 strokes a minute when working at Tregurtha Downs Mine, Marazion. Doubt has been cast on both these claims by Joe Buzza, who drove Robinsons engine between 1926 and 1949. He did not believe it possible for any large pumping engine to achieve such speeds. (46)

The company formed to work Killifreth, in October 1912, had a capital of £100,000, of which £60,000 was paid in shares to purchase the mine, and the remaining £40,000 was to be used as working capital. Captain Leeson was the mine manager. A large proportion of the capital had been spent when factors beyond the control of the owners intervened to stop operations. In August 1914 the Great War broke out, instantly causing the closure of the Franco-Belgian owned Great Wheal Busy, and thereafter closing Killifreth and Wheal Peevor also. Another factor was the dramatic drop in the tin price between 1913 and 1914, from over £120 a ton to just £90. There was also an almost immediate labour shortage, as miners left to volunteer for the armed forces by the thousand. As is usual, the best went first. Even at South Crofty, East Pool and Dolcoath the reduction in the number of skilled miners was soon felt. At first it could be compensated for, by transferring men from development to production, neglecting the essential search for new ore reserves, but eventually, even that failed to keep production up. By the end of the War mines had lost productivity, and by failing to keep up with development, had often destroyed their future prospects also. Newly reopened mines like Wheal Peevor and Killifreth stood no chance in that climate, and the latter closed by the end of 1914, followed by Wheal Peevor in 1916. Between 1914 and 1918 Killifreth was looked after by Captain Arthur Richards. (47)

By 1917 the price of tin was almost back to its pre-War level, and once the War was over it went up rapidly, reaching an average of over £190 a ton. With thousands of former miners returning to Cornwall, including many who had gone abroad before the War, the labour shortage was also over. In October 1918, Killifreth resumed operations, under the management of Captain Ernest Bawden. The 85-inch engine drained the mine to the 70fm level, and there began a careful reassessment of the property by sampling. At the same time, the mine surveyor, J H Buckingham, supervised the reconstruction and repair of dangerous and partially blocked parts of the County Adit system, with major by-pass work at Creegbrawse, Tregonnings and Wheal Busy. The underground manager, J C Gribbin, directed the driving of new development ends and opening of abandoned stopes. (48)

Although the mine was drained to the 70fm level, little production took place below the 40fm level, dur to inadequate hoisting arrangements. The problem had not been sorted out before the tin price again began to fall sharply. The shareholders in the company were dismayed. They had spent large – some thought too large – sums on opening up and refurbishing the mine between the years 1912-14, and now they had spent even more on a second reopening. Oliver Wethered (of Geevor and Dolcoath), the chairman of Killifreth, called in Captain Josiah Paull of South Crofty, to advise on what course to take. Upon the basis of his report, Killifreth was temporarily closed, Wheal Busy was taken over, and there was concentration on arsenic production from Busy's fairly shallow, long-abandoned copper stopes. (49)

From January 1918, Captain Tonkin of Chacewater, had been employing tributers at Wheal Busy, in the old stopes above the County Adit. Tonkin had sold considerable quantities of arsenic to South Crofty for processing. Captain Paull gave a detailed report on Wheal Busy, including the history of its operation since 1718, the number and characteristics of its lodes, its record of arsenic output under Captain Tonkin, and the results of extensive sampling for tin and arsenic. He concluded that as far as arsenic was concerned, it had better prospects than South Crofty, then the biggest producer in Cornwall. The owners of Killifreth did not hesitate once they had read Paull's report. They stopped Hawkes 85-inch engine and turned over completely to arsenic production at Wheal Busy. It did them precious little good, for the price of arsenic dropped thereafter, and Wheal Busy's pumping engine was also stopped. What little activity that continued at the two mines, was in the years between 1923 and 1927, when the whole of the plant of these two ancient mines was put up for sale. Captain Tonkin remained at the helm throughout this final period of working. (50)

Production figures for the period 1809 to 1921 are far from complete, but what figures do exist are quite impressive for such a small mine. Tin raised in Killifreth Woods between 1809 and 1823 realised £42,411. Copper sold by Wood Mine from 1823 to 1853 totalled £123,360. Bewteen 1858 and 1913, Killifreth produced 4,119 tons of black tin. The grade varied, but it was generally between 39 lb and 47 lb per ton, which is better than two percent. It also produced 713 tons of copper ore of about eight percent. Although output figures for the years 1918 to 1921 are sketchy, it is believed that about 3,000 tons of tin ore was raised and dressed. This realised just under sixty tons of black tin. Killifreth also produced seventeen tons of pyrite, twelve tons of mispickel, six tons of ochre and some wolfram. At the average prices of the early 1980s, output from 1809 to 1921, would be valued in excess of £40,000,000. (51)

The year 1927 saw the end of mining at Killifreth and Wheal Busy on any scale, and apart from informal tributers, who moved back into the shallow stopes as they had in 1897, all activity ceased. In February 1928, the machinery of both mines was sold. South Crofty purchased Wheal Busy's 85-inch engine for spares for Robinsons 80-inch engine. It was left in its house until the Second World War, when American army engineers moved into Wheal Busy. The locals tell of how the Americans got the old engine working again, pumping water from the mine to use in their large camp. Unfortunately, the water was heavily contaminated with arsenic and copper, and when used for showering it had a nasty affect upon the soldiers' skin. After the War, South Crofty sold the engine for scrap, and it was broken up. Half of the beam at least remained on site, for in dynamiting it, the scrap metal merchants blew the outside half down the engine shaft. (52)

The 85-inch engine at Hawkes Shaft suffered a similar fate a little earlier, as did the little 22-inch whim engine. In 1943 the Americans blew up both engines, either to remove them or for explosives practice, and apart from destroying two beautiful engines, they did serious damage to the enginehouses. The whim enginehouse was almost completely destroyed, but Hawkes survived in relatively safe condition until the present time. The explosives blasted solid, cast-iron engine supports into the granite walls of Hawkes enginehouse, where they were found in May 1987, by the Manpowers Service Commission labour employed by Carrick District Council to secure and renovate the enginehouse. (53)

Hawkes enginehouse was the first to be renovated by Carrick in a programme to secure these historic mining relics for the future. It is part of a complex of mine buildings that have survived at Killifreth, and it is hoped, will eventually be used to educate the young about their mining heritage, remind adults of an industry until recently so important, and help visitors appreciate Cornwall's great industrial past.

Picture taken in July 1979 by Tony Clarke. The Brunton calciner on the left is part hidden in the undergrowth, with the stamps, Old Sump and Hawkes enginehouses in line. Buckinghams Stack, which was connected to the calciner by a long flue or 'lambreth', is on the right. It had been struck by lightning.

CHARACTERS, LEGENDS & TRAGEDIES

KILLIFRETH, like most old Cornish mines long closed, had its share of legends, stories and characters. It has also had its tragedies. The late Ken Buckingham, for many years parish clerk at Chacewater, whose father was chief surveyor at Killifreth and Wheal Busy, and whose great-grandfather was a mine captain there, has recalled many strange and amusing tales about the place and the characters who worked there. Killifreth has its own story of untouched, hidden wealth. In 1927, just before the two mines were finally 'knacked', the underground manager, John Gribbin, approached John Henry Buckingham, the surveyor, and told him that developers working above the adit level, in the western part of Killifreth, had found the 'richest bunch of tin in Carn Marth district'. Gribbin said that he had 'stilled up the end' with rocks to avoid its discovery. He intended to return and unofficially mine it if the mine closed. A fortnight later the mines did close and were sold up. Neither Gribbin or John Henry ever got the chance to return to the rich end, although neither forgot about it, and both told their respective sons of the exact location.

Over forty years later, a surveyor at Wheal Jane heard the story and enquired of the two men's sons as to its whereabouts. A search was made, and sure enough the stilled up end was found, and the ore was discovered to be just as rich as they had been told. Unfortunately, the ore body lay close to the western boundary of the mine, and ran straight into the neighbouring property. The frequent sampling expeditions to the mine during the last sixty years, have, according to Ken Buckingham, confirmed the idea of untapped wealth there. Few reports have disagreed that there is an abundance of good tin ore awaiting extraction.

John Henry Buckingham was in many ways a larger than life character. He started mining at old Wheal Jane, when he was 15 years old, working with his uncles. On one occasion, whilst 'beating the borer', he missed the drill with his 5 lb hammer, and struck his uncle on the arm. His uncle Mat, infamous for being a hard man with a foul temper, let out a scream of rage, and the boy ran as fast as his guttering candle would let him, along the level. He had not travelled far when the drill steel hit him on the back of his head, rendering him unconscious. When he recovered, he was a little more careful in striking the drill. Later on, he went to work as a miner at the newly reopened Wheal Peevor, while studying mine surveying and assaying at night school. In 1915, when the mine was desperately short of materials, especially timber, the youngster led a strike there, when it was discovered that the mine manager, Captain Curnow, had built an extension on his house with timber taken from the mine. The following week, he had an extra 10s (50p) in his pay packet, but he gave it back to the manager, and said: "You can't buy John Henry Buckingham for ten bob a week, cap'n!"

By the end of the Great War, John Henry had qualified with distinction in surveying and assaying and was appointed chief surveyor at the newly reopened Killifreth Mine. He was responsible not only for routine surveying, but also for the reconstruction and repair of long sections of the County Adit. His name can still be seen on mine plans at the Cornwall Record Office and at Tregothnan. Once a month, he had to inspect the adit system from Halenbeagle to Unity Wood, via Wheal Busy and Killifreth. He had a submersible boat made, so that they could float down the adit, and drag it under water, through low places. The boat was lowered down a shaft at Halenbeagle on the end of a rope, and pulled up an adit shaft at Unity Wood, once the inspection was complete.

Once he realised that Killifreth and Wheal Busy were to close, Buckingham got a job at Tresavean Mine as underground manager, under Captain Faull. He was joined there by several other former Killifreth men, like Albert Harris and Joe Lean, both of Chacewater. In those days miners moved about between mines quite often, sometimes for more money and sometimes just for a change. As mines opened and closed in the 1920s, many men moved out of necessity, sometimes walking or cycling long distances to their new places of employment. One such man, who moved around the mines, was a Lanner character called 'Doctor' Mayne. He was called 'Doctor' because he had a remedy for every ailment and an answer for every criticism. On one occasion he was fired for telling the shiftboss to 'Go to hell', when asked to do a job underground. When the manager, Captain Faull, saw the 'Doctor' in the dry he asked why he was up so early. Mayne told the manager what had happened, and the manager replied that although he was sorry to lose a good miner, he could not go against the shiftboss in this matter. "You apologise, my son, an' I'll take ee back!" When the shiftboss came into the dry at the end of the shift, he demanded to know what Mayne was still doing there. He told the shiftboss what Captain Faull had said, and back came the reply, "Well, go on then, I'm waiting!" After a moment's thought, the 'Doctor' said, "You know I said you could go to 'ell? Well, you've no need to go now!" The shiftboss shook his head and walked away laughing.

On another occasion the 'Doctor' came to work suffering with extreme constipation and a very painful stomach. One of his Chacewater mates gave him a couple of 'Bilkey's pills', which were made by a 'wise man from down to Bissoe'. These apparently contained bitter aloes and were considered by locals to be pretty vicious. The next day 'Doctor' Mayne went underground and looked quite well. His mate, who had noted his new, cheerful state, enquired as to the effect of the pills. "Pills was bleddy marvelous. I'll tell ee what, ol' pard, if'n you never 'ad a 'ole in your arse, they liddle buggers would bore one for ee!"

Another well-remembered Killifreth miner was 'Granfer' Tregonning, who was notorious for winding up his mates. 'Granfer Gonning', as he was known, worked with a group of Chacewater men led by Tommy Jack Oates, who was the tributer. One day 'Granfer Gonning' was taking down loose ground from the hanging wall. He was standing on a flimsy timber platform, about twenty feet (6m) above the floor of the stope, and using a hammer and moyle (chisel). Due to the awkwardness of his situation, 'Granfer' kept dropping the moyle and having to clamber down the staging to retrieve it. Eventually, losing patience, he tied his drill sling, which was round his waist, to the moyle, and for a while it saved his energy. Unfortunately for 'Granfer', the moyle jammed behind a piece of rock, and his violent struggle to get it out, caused the staging upon which he stood to collapse. 'Granfer' was left hanging by his drill sling twenty feet above the pile. Tommy Jack, the taker, took one look at the suspended man and announced to the rest of the pare that it was croust time. Without a word the group of miners trooped out of the stope to the croust seat on the level below, leaving 'Granfer' where he was, screaming for them to help him. Half-an-hour later they returned and carried on drilling as though nothing had happened. Eventually, they climbed up and let the shouting old man down, as he hurled every choice expletive he could think of at them. His mates reckoned he was considerably less irritating thereafter.

Matthew Wicks was a tiny man, hardly five feet tall, and very spare. 'Beating the borer' every day, however, made him extremely strong. He would walk every day up from Chacewater to the mine and then climb the hundreds of feet down to his workplace with the best of them. One day, whilst drilling, Mat missed the end of the drill steel with his 5 lb hammer, and broke his mate's arm. It snapped like a stick. Upon reaching the surface with the injured man, the miners were confronted by the angry manager, who demanded to know what had happened. "Twernt my fault cap'n, man's arm must 'ave bin rotten!" replied the little miner.

When at Tresavean, John Henry Buckingham got a message to look at a shaft that had gone down behind Lanner Village. He was joined in his inspection by Captain Faull, the manager. They were quietly discussing what had to be done, when all of a sudden Captain Faull began shouting at the top of his voice: "I want this shaft capped and fenced right away, Captain Buckingham. Right away. This must be made safe for the children of Lanner, Captain Buckingham, immediately. Today, d'you hear?" and so on. After a minute or two had passed, the two men set off on their walk back toward the count house, and Buckingham said, "What was all that shouting about, cap'n?"

Faull replied: "That's called diplomacy, John Henry, diplomacy. Do you see that old girl down there in that field? In half-an-hour she'll 'ave told all the village what a good man Cap'n Faull is, an' how concerned he is for the safety of the children."

John Henry burst out laughing. "That old lady's a bucca, cap.n. A bloody scarecrow. She waint be tellin' the village anything. It's time you got to wearin' they glasses, because your eyes are getting' worse, Cap'n Faull." The two men walked the rest of the way back laughing uproariously.

After a while some of the Killifreth men at Tresavean heard about the high rates being paid to skilled miners at the newly reopened Kings Down Mine, at Hewas. The pay was high because the locals were clay men and not hard rock miners, so that the owners were paying over the odds to get results. Albert Harris, Joe Lean and other Chacewater men were soon earning high wages, and wrote to John Henry with the news. Underground managers did not earn big wages in those days, so John Henry quit Tresavean and joined his fellow Killifreth miners at Kings Down. He earned well until the manager heard about his qualifications, and he was appointed surveyor and assayer. When the manager had a stroke, Buckingham took over and found that the owners had been misled for months over the value of the tin ore at the mine. He tried all means to get to the bottom of it, and on his death bed the manager confessed that he had 'prilled' the samples with good tin, to make the grades appear higher than they were.

Later, John Henry went to Tincroft Mine to work, which was then part of South Crofty. Whilst employed there he became embroiled in the industrial disputes which broke out at Crofty in the late 1930s. In his battle with the unions he fired some 'red' Welshmen, who he thought were causing the trouble. His widely publicised view on the great 1939 strike at South Crofty, was summed up with his call to "Fire the lot of them!"

A notorious Killifreth character was 'Cunning Dick' Tregonning. He caused irritation and amusement by taking anything left lying about around Chacewater district, to the parish pound at the bottom of Cox Hill. On one occasion he pushed a wheel barrow into the pound, and tethered it among the other 'strays'. Dick normally slept on Killifreth dressing floors and acted as a sort of unpaid, unofficial caretaker and night-watchmen. He was a famous wit and was never short of an answer. One day, whilst standing by Hawkes Shaft the pump came into fork, accompanied by a deep sucking noise that carried 800 feet up the shaft. "Some suction there, cap'n", said Dick, to the mine engineer who was standing nearby.

"No, Dick, that's where you're wrong. That's not suction. There's no such thing in nature as suction. That's atmospheric pressure causing the water to be drawn like that."

Dick thought for a moment, removing his cap and scratching his head with his pipe. "No such thing as suction, mister? No such thing, eh? Well I 'll tell ee what ol' pard, there sure as 'ell was suction the other night when Granny 'Gonnin' emptied out a boil on my arse. I went 'ome an' could 'ardly sit down fer this 'orrible gert boil. Granny 'Gonnin' put an earthenware bottle in the stove, an' 'eated it up till it was red 'ot. She put un over the boil an' threw cold water on it. I tell ee what, mister, thet there bottle was suckin' so 'ard my 'ole arse was inside an' another ten seconds an' I'd o' bin inside meself, if Granny 'adn't smashed thet there bottle with a spallin' 'ammer."

After a slight pause, during which those nearby wiped the tears from their eyes, Dick added, "'Magine me inside thet there bottle, lookin' out. In Truru museem folk 'ld say, "Ere, 'owe'd they get 'e in there?""

Along with the humour Cornish mines have had their share of tragedies, and Killifreth was no exception. The accident to William Trelease, on December 2nd 1891, had its ironic side also. Trelease was rising over the 30fm level on contract. He was a tutworker, which meant he was paid by the footage he advanced his rise upwards. Rising or raising has long been considered one of the most dangerous of mining tasks, and in recent years few jobs at South Crofty have produced as many serious accidents. On December 2nd William Trelease was doing what was considered a 'safe' job. He was engaged with several other miners in lowering a roller down a shaft with an air winch. His job was to look after the slack rope, but he allowed it to get too loose and it caught his leg around the winch barrel. By the time his mates could release him, it was apparent that he was very badly injured, for his leg was smashed above the knee. The alarm was raised and Chacewater 'ambulance' was rushed to the mine to convey him to Redruth Miners Hospital. The ambulance, until the 1950s kept in Chacewater Market House, was built like a large, old-fashioned child's pram. It had four big wheels, boat springs, and the frame was covered by two large planks. As soon as the alarm was raised men rushed the ambulance to Killifreth, whilst others ran along the road to Redruth, to set up relay stations. Trelease was placed on the planks and the contraption was rushed at high speed toward the hospital, fresh men taking over as those pushing tired. By the time the conveyance approached West End Hill, there was a large crowd of running, sweating, gasping miners accompanying the injured man. But, it was all to no avail, for when they arrived, it was discovered that William was already dead.

For over half a century Killifreth represented mining at Chacewater, for it was almost the sole survivor of the industry upon which the village was built. Tragedies like that of William Trelease, as well as characters like 'Cunning Dick' and 'Granfer' Tregonning, helped cement the village into a tight-knit community. Humour and sudden death were shared experiences. The history of Cornish mining is not just about managers, production figures, shaft sinking and great Cornish engines, it is also the story of the men and women themselves. Miners, tin and copper dressers, engine drivers, timbermen, carpenters, blacksmiths, bal maidens and all the rest, played their part in the long and fascinating story of mining at Killifreth. When the buildings are mere ruins, the mighty engines long gone for scrap and the names of the managers and adventurers long-forgotten, it is the host of unnamed miners who should be celebrated and their achievements never forgotten.

Appendix A

Engines

1865. 12-inch rotative pumping engine at Engine Shaft (Old Sump)

1873. 50-inch pumping engine at Engine Shaft. Purchased from Wheal Daniell for £1,000 with 11 ton boiler. Erected at Wheal Daniell in October 1871 & hardly used.

1876. 32-inch stamps engine. Purchased with two 16 head stamps axles & buddles, etc for £560.

1891/2. 80-inch pumping engine at Hawkes (Richards) Shaft. Bought from North Treskerby with balance bob, whim, rope, rods, etc for £575. Built in 1860 for Wheal Falmouth & Sperries; sold to Lanyons 1869; sold to N Treskerby for £800; broken up after 1897 closure of Killifreth.

1892. Whim engine. Sold by Killifreth to Par Mine (Tregrehan Consols) for £45.

1892/5. 22-inch whim engine. Erected by F W Michell between Hawkes & Engine shafts, to draw from either shaft.

1893/5. Stamps engine re-cylindered from 32-inch to 36-inch. Stamps doubled to 64 heads.

1892/5. 12-inch cylinder capstan engine, erected by F W Michell.

1913/14. 85-inch pumping engine erected at Hawkes Shaft. Made by Perran Foundry in 1871. Worked on Welsh lead mines for 40 years before going to Killifreth. At Great Fron Fownog Mine, Flintshire, allegedly broke large engine record with 14 strokes a minute. It pumped 80,000 gallons an hour.

1913/14. Whim engine erected on west side of Hawkes Shaft.

1893/4. American type 'safety cage' installed at Killifreth. First to be used in Cornwall. Designed and constructed by Sara's Foundry, Redruth.

Appendix B

Managers/Pursers/Mine Captains.

Managers:

1809-23	William Paul
1858-62	Joel Higgins
1863-79	George E Tremayne (Sparg calls him John)
1880-93	Captain John Michell
1893-97	Captain R A James
1897-98	Oliver Northey
1898-1907	William Burrows
1912-14	Captain Leeson
1914-18	Captain Arthur Richards
1918-23	E R Bawden
1923-27	Captain Tonkin

Pursers/Secretaries:

1859-71	Edward H Hawke
1871-72	Thomas Gough
1872-92	John Tregonning
1892-97	Thomas F Trounson

Mine Captains/Agents:

1859-64	Captain John Whitburn
1863-68	Captain Alexander Nancarrow
1872-76	Captain Thomas Gough
1872-74	Captain William Buckingham
1872-77	Captain John Paul
1879-80	Captain John Michell
1880-81	Captain Joseph Paull
1881-82	Captain John Trevethan
1881-87	Captain Joseph Tamblyn
1891-93	Captain R A James
1894-95	Philip Michell
1894-95	J W Bryant
1887-97	Captain Oliver Northey
1918-27	J C Gribbin 'Underground foreman'
1918-25	Captain Tonkin

Mine Engineers:

1873-97	F W Michell (Engineers) of Redruth.

Appendix C

Numbers Employed.

Year.	Underground.	Surface.	Total.
1865			30
1878	61	29	90
1879	52	25	77
1880	42	15	57
1881	51	26	77
1882	90	68	158
1883	119	64	183
1884	106	51	157
1885	105	49	154
1886	99	44	143
1887	102	36	138
1888	111	47	158
1889	108	45	153
1890	103	41	144
1891	122	55	177
1892	120	83	203
1893	164	60	224
1894	183	98	281
1895	185	82	267
1896	138	75	213
1897	94	59	153
1898	33	8	41
1899	28	5	33
1900	19	1	20
1901	2	5	28
1902	8	1	9
1903	4	-	4
1904	2	2	4
1905	5	1	6
1906	2	2	4
1907	-	1	1
1911	4	-	4
1912	2	-	2
1913	18	43	61

Appendix D
Killifreth Production in Pounds Sterling.

Year	Tin	Copper	Arsenic
1809	£43		
1810	£5931		
1811	£1593		
1812	£59		
1813	£1528		
1814	£6759		
1815	£3228		
1816	£1163		
1817	£2785		
1818	£4376		
1819	£3908		
1820	£2061		
1821	£2633		
1822	£103		
1823	£40	£6850	
1824		£2887	
1825		£1185	
1826		£1066	
1827		£1033	
1828		£456	
1829		£1747	
1830		£2684	
1831		£3358	
1832		£6476	
1833		£12015	
1834		£9831	
1835		£6996	
1836		£9344	
1837		£8061	
1838		£8839	
1839		£11223	
1840		£10923	
1841		£14962	
1842		£2023	
1853		£1395	
1858	£18	£1236	
1859		£1131	
1860	£140		

Year	Tin	Copper	Arsenic
1866		£52	
1873	£4260		£13
1874	£2085		£7
1875	£975		
1876	£3744	£84	£110
1877	£3881	£2188	£80
1878	£950	£305	
1879	£1516		
1880	£460	£16	£30
1880	£815		
1881	£14528	£29	£36
1883	£13260	£25	£40
1884	£7059	£34	£39
1885	£8495		
1886	£8985		£9
1887	£7131		
1888	£8030		
1889	£7545		
1890	£8212		
1891	£14596		
1892	£16846		
1892	£17617		£239
1893	£15938		£471
1894	£11873		£551
1895	£9847		£447
1896	£5089		£543
1897	£808		
1898	£726		
1899	£853		
1900	£797		
1901	£559		
1902	£299		
1903	£217		
1904	£212		
1905	£78		
1906	£6		
1911	£160		
1912	£50		

REFERENCES

1. William Pryce. Corn-Britannica (1790)
2. B Cunliffe. Pytheas the Greek (2001) pp.73-115; C H Oldfather Doidorus of Sicily (1939) pp.142,255; Allen Buckley. The Story of Mining in Cornwall (2007) pp.12-21
3. HC 66 p.86 (Aug.27 1517) RIC,Truro
4. HA/3/12 (Feb.1523) RIC
5. Henderson vol.3 p.105 RIC
6. Star Chamber Cases (1517) vol.xxvii 1; xxi 97; Henderson vol.3 p.256 RIC
7. HG/6/1 (Nov.24 1615)RIC
8. HG/6/3 (July 3 1617) RIC
9. HG/6/12 (Nov.3 1631) RIC
10. HG/6/13 (June 11 1639) RIC
11. HG/6/20 (April 26 1676) RIC
12. R T Gunther. Early Science in Oxford (1925) vol.3 pp.497-9
13. William Pryce. Mineralogia Cornubiensis (1778) pp.277-9, 286,287
14. W H Pascoe. CCC: The History of the Cornish Copper Company (1981) pp.21-23
15. E R Bawden. Killifreth Mine, Cornwall Mining Magazine (May 1929) pp.279-286; Killifreth Estate Map (1920), Private Collection
16. J A Buckley. The Great County Adit (2000) pp.137,138
17. TL 97 (Wheal Unity Cost Book July 1772) CRO, Truro; Buckley (2000) pp.40-42
18. County Adit Cost Book (1858), Private Collection
19. Geology of Killifreth based on E R Bawden Mining Magazine (May 1929) pp.279-286; Captain Charles Thomas of Dolcoath Letter (June 2 1854); Theophilus Michell Letter (June 10 1854), Private Collection
20. DDX 475/14,15,17 CRO; Poldice Deep Adit Cost Book (1806), Private Collection
21. Richard Thomas. Report on a Survey of the Mining Region from Camborne to Chacewater (1819) p.64
22. Theophilus Michell Letter Books (July 1 1851& Sept.20 1853), Private Collection
23. Killifreth Mine Reports Private Collection; Ken Buckingham, Pers.Comm.
24. Estate & Mine Accounts, Private Collection
25. J Y Watson. Compendium of British Mining (1843) p.29
26. Theophilus Michell Letter Books, Private Collection; Killifreth Mine Reports, Private Collection
27. Thomas Spargo. The Mines of Cornwall: IV Redruth Area (1865) p.8
28. Killifreth Mine Reports (1870-96)
29. Killifreth Mine Reports (1870-96)
30. Allen Buckley. Dolcoath: A History (2010) p.315
31. James Bryant Letter Books (July & November 1880), Private Collection
32. James Bryant Letter Books (Nov.29 1880) pp.194,195, Private Collection
33. John Tregonning Letter (April 1884), Private Collection
34. James Bryant Letter Books

35. Robert Symons. Gazeteer of Cornwall (1884)
36. Killifreth Mine Reports (1860-90), Private Collection
37. Buckley (2010) p.313; D B Barton. Tin Mining & Smelting in Cornwall (1967) pp.199,220; T A Morrison. Cornwall's Central Mines: Southern District (1983) pp.45,51
38. Herbert Thomas. Mining Interviews (1896) pp.192-205
39. Killifreth Mine Reports (1890-96), Private Collection; Ken Buckingham Pers. Comm.; Mining Journal Letter from T F Trounson (Aug.15 1894); Letter Charles Jenkin (May 1896), Private Collection
40. J H Collins. Observations on the West of England Mining Region (1912) p.515; MJ (Aug.14 1897); MJ (Oct.23 1897)
41. Thomas (1896) pp.192-205
42. MJ (Aug.14 1897) Letter from Mr Vergo of Chacewater
43. MJ (Sept.25 1897)
44. MJ (Sept.27 1897)
45. James Bryant Letter Book, Private Collection
46. Joseph Tamblyn, Manager of East Pool, Report (June 8 1906), Private Collection; Trevithick Society Newsletter No.45; Personnel communications from John H Trounson, Kenneth Brown & Joseph Buzza
47. Captain Josiah Paull, Manager of South Crofty, Report (1915) CMDA 1/29 CRO; E R Bawden Mining Magazine (May 1929) p.279
48. Ken Buckingham Pers.Comm.
49. E R Bawden Reports (Dec.30 1919 & June 15 1920) Private Collection
50. Bawden Mining Magazine (May 1929) pp.279-286; Josiah Paull's Reports on Killifreth & Wheal Busy (1920 & 1921) CMDA 1 CRO; MJ (1919) p.626; MJ (1920) p.136; MJ (1921) p.17; MJ (1923) p.185; MJ (1924) p.165
51. Captain Josiah Paull Report (Jan.27 1925) CMDA CRO; Edgar Trestrail Report (1927) CMDA CRO
52. Ken Buckingham Pers.Comm.
53. Ken Buckingham Pers.Comm.